THE ROSARY

A Worried Parent Prays

Andrew Jerome Yeung

THE ROSARY

A Worried Parent Prays

Andrew Jerome Yeung

The Ave Maria Centre of Peace
P.O. Box 489, Station U
Toronto, Ontario, M8Z 5Y8
Canada

Canadian Cataloguing in Publication Data

Yeung, Andrew Jerome, 1938-
  The rosary: a worried parent prays

ISBN 0-9684895-8-3

1. Rosary. 2. Mysteries of the Rosary. 3. Parents
— Prayer-books and devotions — English. 4.
Catholic Church — Prayer-books and devotions
— English. I. Ave Maria Centre of Peace. II.
Title.

BX2163.Y48 2000   242'.74   C00-930764-8

Printed and bound in Canada
by Ave Maria Centre of Peace

Two of the author's other books:

LIVE JESUS' GOSPEL, NOW!

PARENTS, PEACE

Available at
Ave Maria Centre of Peace
P.O. 489, Station U
Toronto, Ontario, M8Z 5Y8
Canada

Acknowledgments

In this work, any passage designated NJB is an excerpt from THE NEW JERUSALEM BIBLE, copyright (c) 1985 by Darton, Longman & Todd, Ltd. and Doubleday, a division of Random House, Inc. Reprinted by permission.

Scripture excerpts marked NAB in this work are taken from the NEW AMERICAN BIBLE with Revised New Testament and Revised Psalms (c) 1991, 1986, 1970 Confraternity of Christian Doctrine, Washington, D.C. Used with permission. All rights reserved. No part of the NEW AMERICAN BIBLE may be reproduced in any form without permission in writing from the copyright owner.

Excerpt taken from *Catechism of Catholic Church*, Copyright © Concacan Inc. — LIBRERIA EDITRICE VATICANA, 1994, for the English translation in Canada. All rights reserved. Used by permission of the Canadian Conference of Catholic Bishops, Ottawa, Canada.

Nihil Obstat	His Eminence
&	Aloysius Cardinal Ambrozic
Imprimatur	Archbishop of Toronto
Censor Deputatus	Rev. Fr. Thomas R. Harding

Table of Contents

FOREWORD

The most popular devotion given to us by the Blessed Virgin Mary is the Rosary. It came from her in a private revelation to St. Dominic, the founder of the Order of Preachers — the Dominicans. St. Dominic was born in Spain in 1170, and died in 1221.

Tradition tells us that the Mother of God appeared to St. Dominic and asked him to spread the Holy Rosary as a powerful means of counteracting the Albigensian Heresy in the 12th and 13th centuries (and ultimately to quell error and vice in every age). It was given to the Dominicans because this Order had been raised up to combat the heresies of Medieval Europe. The false doctrines in that period of history had a common thread: they denied that Our Lord took human flesh of his Mother. They regarded matter as something evil and they could not believe that the Son of God took on himself human flesh and that he was born after the manner of man.

Accordingly, it was the Birth of Jesus Christ which had to be preached, and the Incarnation was the string which bound all the prayers of the Rosary together. The Rosary is sometimes referred to as Our Lady's prayer, but it is not her life primarily which is the subject of our meditation during the fifteen decades — it is the life of her Divine Son, especially that He became man, that is, the meeting of the Divine with the human. This is the point of the Incarnation, and it is the point of the Holy Rosary.

The devotion is quite cleverly organized. First, you have a Rosary which you cherish. Second, you have its beads to occupy your fingers. Thirdly, you have the main prayers, the "I Believe in God", the "Our Father", the "Hail Mary" and the "Glory be to the Father" to occupy your lips. Finally, the Joyful, Sorrowful and Glorious Mysteries of the life of Jesus Christ occupy your mind and heart.

What a perfect prayer! It is easy to say with family and friends, and it provides all the steps in our community prayer. It is also easy to say alone — at home, in the car, on the subway or bus when you just want to pray for fifteen minutes or so. (I find it hard to recite the Rosary in bed because I tend to fall asleep. Then some say the Angels finish it for you, but I wouldn't count on that habitually.)

The Rosary is not just for the simple or uneducated. It is a great prayer for everyone.

I often hear people say they do not like the Rosary because it is repetitive and boring. I have said that myself — mea culpa, mea culpa, mea maxima culpa. However, I am getting to like it in my old age. As the German saying goes: "Too soon old, too late smart." I should try to say the fifteen decades every day in my advancing years.

I wish to thank my friend, Andrew, for sending me the manuscript of his latest work: *THE ROSARY, A Worried Parent Prays.* This is his fourth. I am quite impressed and inspired by his writings. The booklet will be a great help not only to parents but to all Catholics. It will be well received by all. I am honoured to have my words included here.

Rev. Thomas R. Harding, B.A., M.A., Ph.D.
Priest of the Archdiocese of Toronto

INTRODUCTION

What is the purpose of the Rosary?

The Rosary is a means for us to become more closely united to Jesus and Mary; through this prayer we stay in touch with their earthly and heavenly lives, and in so doing we hope to grow in understanding of — and thankfulness for — God's unfailing love, a love proven by the incarnation, suffering, death, resurrection and ascension of Jesus, by the action of the Holy Spirit, by the intimate co-operation of mother Mary and the participation of the angels and saints.

Chapter One presents a fruitful way for an apprehensive parent to pray. Herein lies the chief reason for the existence of this booklet. Those who are familiar with the Rosary and do not wish to read the other chapters but decide to pray in the manner described, will have already benefited themselves — and anyone else for whom they offer up petitions.

Chapter Two lists the assurances Our Lady gave to those who recite the Rosary.

Chapter Three, the longest, contains the Scripture quotations connected with the fifteen Mysteries. (One text is from the *Catechism of the Catholic Church*.)

Chapter Four shows the beginner how the Rosary is prayed. It is indeed an excellent devotion, but should not be said mechanically. For this reason a variety of traditional spiritual activities is reviewed.

Chapter Five explains briefly the Church's teaching on indulgences, and outlines some which can be obtained by the faithful who, while in a state of grace, recite the Rosary and other prayers associated with it.

Chapter One

A Worried Parent's Rosary

The Rosary is a remarkably adaptable prayer. It can be used as an aid for contemplation, meditation, blessing, adoration, petition, intercession, thanksgiving and praise. The following illustrates how a father or mother, solicitous about the salvation of the children, can pray with faith, hope and love.

The Scripture quotations are taken from the passages collected together in Chapter Three (unless otherwise indicated).

Opening Prayer

O my God, I beg of you to listen to this humble prayer offered for the eternal welfare of my family. Please, Lord, bring my children back to you in holiness and peace. I ask this in the name of Jesus, in union with the Holy Spirit, through the Immaculate Heart of Mary, and with all your angels and saints. Amen.

(A) The Joyful Mysteries

1. The first Joyful Mystery
The Annunciation

The angel Gabriel assured Mary: "Nothing will be impossible for God." (Luke 1:37, NAB)

With you, Lord, all that is good can be accomplished: from the conversion of the most hardened sinners to the unraveling of problems that seem to have no solutions.

Loving Father, you created my children but have not abandoned them to deal with their burdens, weaknesses and sins completely on their own. Thank you for your plan of Redemption, and for the gift of your Son. "He will save his people from their sins." (Matthew 1:21, NAB)

2. The second Joyful Mystery
The Visitation

In her "Magnificat" Mary enunciated this consoling truth about God: "His mercy is from age to age to those who fear him." (Luke 1:50, NAB)

Holy Spirit, your mercy does not stop with me; it extends to every generation, to my children, and to their descendants.

Thank you for the many transformations you will draw forth from them as the years go by.

3. The third Joyful Mystery
The Birth of Jesus

On the night Jesus was born, an angel appeared to the shepherds in the neighbouring fields and said, "Do not be afraid; for behold, I proclaim to you good news of great joy that will be for all the people. For today in the city of David a savior has been born for you who is Messiah and Lord." (Luke 2:10-11, NAB)

Dear Jesus, your good news of salvation is for the entire human race — the just and the unjust, those who go to church and those who do not, the ones who know they need you and the ones who ignore your very existence.

From my youth you have corrected me in gradual stages, how can I suppose you will not do the same for my sons and daughters? You are my Saviour; you are theirs too.

Lord, help me not to be afraid but to trust you in joy.

4. The fourth Joyful Mystery
The Presentation

At the temple, holding baby Jesus in his arms, Simeon blessed God, saying, "Now, Master, you may let your servant go in peace, according to your word, for my eyes have seen your salvation." (Luke 2:29-30, NAB)

Lord, just as Simeon commended himself to you in peaceful resignation, let me rest in you now as I lay at your feet all my concerns for the children.

In times of difficulties, or when tempted to despair, may I always call on your holy name: "Jesus, Master, we need you."

5. The fifth Joyful Mystery
Finding of Jesus in the Temple

On the third day, Jesus' parents located him in Jerusalem. His mother complained, "My child, why have you done this to us? See how worried your father and I have been, looking for you." (Luke 2:48, NJB)

Joseph and Mary, if you searched with so much anxiety for Jesus, the perfect son, how much more are you going after those who have really gone astray! Thank you for your participation in pursuing my children and leading them back to the Lord.

(B) The Sorrowful Mysteries

1. The first Sorrowful Mystery
The Agony in the Garden

At Gethsemane, Jesus, acutely aware of the torment awaiting him at the crucifixion, began to feel severe anguish, distress, and grief. "He was in such agony and he prayed so fervently that his sweat became like drops of blood falling on the ground." (Luke 22:44, NAB) And going on a little further he fell on his face and begged, "Abba, Father!... For you everything is possible. Take this cup away from me. But let it be as you, not I, would have it." (Mark 14:36, NJB)

Jesus, I suspect what terrified you most was the tremendous pain from the driving of the nails into your hands and feet. Every time I try to visualize it happening to me I recoil in utter horror. Thank you, dear Friend, for deciding in our favour, for your determination to make reparation for the sins we committed, for submitting to the Father's will, knowing thereby no one in my family would perish.

2. The second Sorrowful Mystery
The Scourging at the Pillar

"Pilate then had Jesus taken away and scourged." (John 19:1, NJB)

Jesus, Isaiah prophesied this about you: "He was being wounded for our rebellions, crushed because of our guilt; the punishment reconciling us fell on him, and we have been healed by his bruises." (Isaiah 53:5, NJB)

St. Peter affirmed the prophesy: "By his wounds you have been healed." (1 Peter 2:24, NAB)

Thank you, Lord, for healing my children.

3. The third Sorrowful Mystery
The Crowning with Thorns

"And they stripped him and put a scarlet cloak round him, and having twisted some thorns into a crown they put this on his head and placed a reed in his right hand. To make fun of him they knelt to him saying, 'Hail, king of the Jews!' And they spat on him and took the reed and struck him on the head with it." (Matthew 27:28-30, NJB)

God of all creation, you accepted insults and insolence in silence for the conversion of my children. I do not fully comprehend the dynamics of this course of action, but sometimes it may be wise to follow your example and do the same in my own home.

4. The fourth Sorrowful Mystery
The Carrying of the Cross

"As they were leading him away they seized on a man, Simon from Cyrene, who was coming in from the country, and made him shoulder the cross and carry it behind Jesus." (Luke 23:26, NJB)

Lord, like Simon, I will take up the cross after you. You gave so much of yourself to the children, I will also do my part for them. No matter what troubling situation they may be in, however uncomfortable I may feel from disruptions, emotional strain, heartaches, inconvenience, whatever needs to be spent — time, energy, money — I will be there for them, in quiet support, in prayerful supplication, in loving tenderness.

Scripture tells us:

"Above all, let your love for one another be intense, because love covers a multitude of sins." (I Peter 4:8, NAB)

"Love covers all offenses." (Proverbs 10:12, NAB)

5. The fifth Sorrowful Mystery
The Crucifixion and Death of Jesus

On the cross Jesus implored, "Father, forgive them, they know not what they do." (Luke 23:34, NAB)

One of the two thieves said to him, "Jesus, remember me when you come into your kingdom." He replied to him, "Amen, I say to you, today you will be with me in Paradise." (Luke 23:42-43, NAB)

Lord, thank you for forgiveness. Thank you for mercy. Truly St. Paul was right in stating, "Where sin increased, grace overflowed all the more." (Romans 5:20, NAB)

And, just in case my children have not asked, I now do so on their behalf: "Father, forgive them, they know not what they do. Jesus, remember them when you come into your kingdom."

(C) The Glorious Mysteries

1. The first Glorious Mystery
The Resurrection

The risen Christ pointed out to Thomas, "You believe because you can see me. Blessed are those who have not seen and yet believe." (John 20:29, NJB)

Jesus, my Lord and my God, at this moment I detect no visible signs of spiritual improvement in my children, but I must learn to believe in the absolute power of the suffering, death and resurrection of the Son of God to bring about their salvation.

God the Father, thank you for allowing them to rise from death. Thank you for the gift of everlasting life.

2. The second Glorious Mystery
The Ascension

"And so the Lord Jesus, after he had spoken to them, was taken up into heaven; there at the right hand of God he took his place." (Mark 16:19, NJB)

"It is Christ Jesus who died, rather, was raised, who also is at the right hand of God, who indeed intercedes for us." (Romans 8:34, NAB) In the presence of the Father, Lord Jesus, you plead constantly for my children. For you love them; you love them much more than I do, far deeper than I can imagine. "For I am convinced that neither death, nor life, nor angels, nor principalities, nor present things, nor future things, nor powers, nor height, nor depth, nor any other creature will be able to separate us from the love of God in Christ Jesus our Lord." (Romans 8:38-39, NAB)

3. The third Glorious Mystery
The Descent of the Holy Spirit

On Pentecost day, Peter reminded the multitude about God's great promise to give the Holy Spirit to his people: "'In the last days — the Lord declares — I shall pour out my Spirit on all humanity.'" (Acts 2:17, NJB)

Peter continued: "The promise that was made is for you and your children, and for all those who are far away, for all those whom the Lord our God is calling to himself." (Acts 2:39, NJB)

Holy Spirit, thank you for coming to my children. Thank you for calling them. I know you will instruct them well because Jesus said, "The

Holy Spirit, whom the Father will send in my name, will teach you everything." (John 14:26, NJB) Lord of Wisdom, under your inspiration, and at an hour known to you, they will respond, they will come to their senses. They will leave the place of sin, and get up and return to the Father.

On that day, like the parent in the parable of the prodigal son, I will jump for joy and exult with all my being. I will cry out in ecstatic jubilation, "Let us celebrate! For my children were dead and have come back to life. They were lost, and are found." (See Luke 15:23-24)

Jesus had insisted, "I tell you, in just the same way there will be more joy in heaven over one sinner who repents than over ninety-nine right-eous people who have no need of repentance." (Luke 15:7, NAB)

4. The fourth Glorious Mystery
The Assumption of Mary into Heaven

"The Assumption of the Blessed Virgin is a sin-gular participation in her Son's Resurrection and an anticipation of the resurrection of other Christians." Her prayers "will deliver our souls from death." (*Catechism of the Catholic Church:* #966)

O Blessed Virgin, thank you that you do not forget my children in your celestial glory. Thank you for keeping them in your prayers. Dear Mary, full of grace, profoundly humble, unselfish, and grateful to God, I believe you will not rest until you have shared all your graces with every single one of your sons and daughters — so ardently does your motherly heart desire their resurrection into heaven.

5. The fifth Glorious Mystery
The Coronation of Mary as Queen of Heaven and Earth

Our Lady was "exalted by the Lord as Queen over all things, so that she might be the more fully conformed to her Son, the Lord of lords and conqueror of sin and death." (*Catechism of the Catholic Church:* #966)

Heavenly Queen, we welcome your reign over us. As Jesus advanced in wisdom and in favour before God while under your authority at Nazareth, I ask of you to also guide my children so that they will grow to be most pleasing to the Father, their Creator and victorious King.

Closing Prayer

Father, Jesus, Holy Spirit, thank you for taking care of my children and all your people. Thank you for your steadfast love.

Mother Mary, the angels and saints, thank you for your whole-hearted co-operation with the divine plan.

Thank you, God, for blessing me personally. Please continue to increase in me your gifts of faith, hope, and love. Continue to increase in me your gifts of understanding and peace. I will include other families in my intentions each time I pray the most holy Rosary.

Chapter Two

Our Lady's Promises

In the 13th and 15th century respectively, Mother Mary made the following commitments to St. Dominic and Blessed Alan de la Roche.

1. Whoever shall faithfully serve me by the recitation of the Rosary shall receive signal graces.

2. I promise my special protection and the greatest graces to all those who shall recite the Rosary.

3. The Rosary shall be a powerful armour against Hell. It will destroy vice, decrease sin, and defeat heresies.

4. It will cause virtue and good works to flourish; it will obtain for souls the abundant mercy of God; it will withdraw the hearts of men from the love of the world and its vanities and will lift them to the desire for eternal things. Oh, that souls would sanctify themselves by this means.

5. The soul which recommends itself to me by the recitation of the Rosary, shall not perish.

6. Whoever shall recite the Rosary devoutly, applying himself to the consideration of its sacred mysteries, shall never be conquered by misfortune. God will not chastise him in his justice; he shall not perish by an unprovided death; if he be just, he shall remain in the grace of God and become worthy of eternal life.

7. Whoever shall have a true devotion to the Rosary shall not die without the Sacraments of the Church.

8. Those who are faithful to reciting the Rosary shall have during their life and at their death the light of God and the plenitude of his graces; at the moment of death, they shall participate in the merits of the saints in Paradise.

9. I shall deliver from Purgatory those who have been devoted to the Rosary.

10. The faithful children of the Rosary shall merit a high degree of glory in Heaven.

11. You shall obtain all you ask of me by the recitation of the Rosary.

12. All those who propagate the Holy Rosary shall be aided by me in their necessities.

13. I have obtained from my Divine Son that all the advocates of the Rosary shall have for intercessors the entire Celestial Court during their life and at the hour of death.

14. All who recite the Rosary are my sons, and brothers of my only Son, Jesus Christ.

15. Devotion to my Rosary is a great sign of predestination.

Chapter Three

The Scripture Texts

Here are most of the readings involved directly in the Rosary. They are mainly from the Gospels. One excerpt comes from the *Catechism of the Catholic Church*; it describes Our Lady's Assumption into Heaven, and her exaltation as Queen over all things.

It is good to be very familiar with these passages because we will not always have them in front of us every time the Rosary is said. They should be reviewed at least once a year. A schedule for doing this would be according to the liturgical cycle. For example, we can study the Joyful Mysteries on the appropriate days in Advent and during the Christmas and New Year season. We can concentrate on the Sorrowful Mysteries during Lent and Holy Week. Then at Easter time, Pentecost, and throughout the month of August, we can look at the Glorious Mysteries. The feast of the Assumption of Mary is on August 15th, and a week later we celebrate her Coronation as Queen of Heaven and earth.

The Joyful Mysteries
1. The Annunciation

In the sixth month, the angel Gabriel was sent from God to a town of Galilee called Nazareth, to a virgin betrothed to a man named Joseph, of the house of David, and the virgin's name was Mary. And coming to her, he said, "Hail, favored one! The Lord is with you." But she was greatly troubled at what was said and pondered what sort of greeting this might be. Then the angel said to her, "Do not be afraid, Mary, for you have found favor with God. Behold, you will conceive in your womb and bear a son, and you shall name him Jesus. He will be great and will be called Son of the Most High, and the Lord God will give him the throne of David his father, and he will rule over the house of Jacob forever, and of his kingdom there will be no end." But Mary said to the angel, "How can this be, since I have no relations with a man?" And the angel said to her in reply, "The holy Spirit will come upon you, and the power of the Most High will overshadow you. Therefore the child to be born will be called holy, the Son of God. And behold, Elizabeth, your relative, has also conceived a son in her old age, and this is the sixth month for her who was called barren; for nothing will be impossible for God." Mary said, "Behold, I am the handmaid of the Lord. May it be done to me according to your word." Then the angel departed from her. (Luke 1:26-38, NAB)

2. The Visitation

During those days Mary set out and traveled to the hill country in haste to a town of Judah, where she entered the house of Zechariah and greeted Elizabeth. When Elizabeth heard Mary's greeting, the infant leaped in her womb, and Elizabeth, filled with the holy Spirit, cried out in a loud voice and said, "Most blessed are you among women, and blessed is the fruit of your womb. And how does this happen to me, that the mother of my Lord should come to me? For at the moment the sound of your greeting reached my ears, the infant in my womb leaped for joy. Blessed are you who believed that what was spoken to you by the Lord would be fulfilled."

And Mary said:

"My soul proclaims the greatness of the Lord;

  my spirit rejoices in God my savior.

For he has looked upon his handmaid's lowliness;

  behold, from now on will all ages call me blessed.

The Mighty One has done great things for me,

  and holy is his name.

His mercy is from age to age

  to those who fear him.

He has shown might with his arm,

dispersed the arrogant of mind and heart.

He has thrown down the rulers from their thrones

but lifted up the lowly.

The hungry he has filled with good things;

the rich he has sent away empty.

He has helped Israel his servant,

remembering his mercy,

according to his promise to our fathers,

to Abraham and to his descendants forever."

Mary remained with her about three months and then returned to her home. (Luke 1:39-56, NAB)

3. The Birth of Jesus

In those days a decree went out from Caesar Augustus that the whole world should be enrolled. This was the first enrollment, when Quirinius was governor of Syria. So all went to be enrolled, each to his own town. And Joseph too went up from Galilee from the town of Nazareth to Judea, to the city of David that is called Bethlehem, because he was of the house and family of David, to be enrolled with Mary, his betrothed, who was with child. While they were there, the time came for her to have her child, and she gave birth to her firstborn son. She wrapped him in swaddling clothes and laid him in a manger, because there was no room for them in the inn.

Now there were shepherds in that region living in the fields and keeping the night watch over their flock. The angel of the Lord appeared to them and the glory of the Lord shone around them, and they were struck with great fear. The angel said to them, "Do not be afraid; for behold, I proclaim to you good news of great joy that will be for all the people. For today in the city of David a savior has been born for you who is Messiah and Lord. And this will be a sign for you: you will find an infant wrapped in swaddling clothes and lying in a manger." And suddenly there was a multitude of the heavenly host with the angel, praising God and saying:

"Glory to God in the highest
  and on earth peace to those on whom his
  favor rests."

When the angels went away from them to heaven, the shepherds said to one another, "Let us go, then, to Bethlehem to see this thing that has taken place, which the Lord has made known to us." So they went in haste and found Mary and Joseph, and the infant lying in the manger. When they saw this, they made known the message that had been told them about this child. All who heard it were amazed by what had been told them by the shepherds. And Mary kept all these things, reflecting on them in her heart. Then the shepherds returned, glorifying and praising God for all they had heard and seen, just as it had been told to them. (Luke 2:1-20, NAB)

4. The Presentation

When the days were completed for their purification according to the law of Moses, they took him up to Jerusalem to present him to the Lord, just as it is written in the law of the Lord, "Every male that opens the womb shall be consecrated to the Lord," and to offer the sacrifice of "a pair of turtledoves or two young pigeons," in accordance with the dictate in the law of the Lord.

Now there was a man in Jerusalem whose name was Simeon. This man was righteous and devout, awaiting the consolation of Israel, and the holy Spirit was upon him. It had been revealed to him by the holy Spirit that he should not see death before he had seen the Messiah of the Lord. He came in the Spirit into the temple; and when the parents brought in the child Jesus to perform the custom of the law in regard to him, he took him into his arms and blessed God, saying:

"Now, Master, you may let your servant go
     in peace, according to your word,
   for my eyes have seen your salvation,
     which you prepared in sight of all the peoples,
   a light for revelation to the Gentiles,
     and glory for your people Israel."
(Luke 2:22-32, NAB)

As the child's father and mother were wondering at the things that were being said about him, Simeon blessed them and said to Mary his mother, "Look, he is destined for the fall and for the rise of many in Israel, destined to be a sign that is opposed — and a sword will pierce your soul too — so that the secret thoughts of many may be laid bare."

There was a prophetess, too, Anna the daughter of Phanuel, of the tribe of Asher. She was well on in years. Her days of girlhood over, she had been married for seven years before becoming a widow. She was now eighty-four years old and never left the Temple, serving God night and day with fasting and prayer. She came up just at that moment and began to praise God; and she spoke of the child to all who looked forward to the deliverance of Jerusalem. (Luke 2:33-38, NJB)

5. Finding of Jesus in the Temple

Every year his parents used to go to Jerusalem for the feast of the Passover. When he was twelve years old, they went up for the feast as usual. When the days of the feast were over and they set off home, the boy Jesus stayed behind in Jerusalem without his parents knowing it. They assumed he was somewhere in the party, and it was only after a day's journey that they went to look for him among their relations and acquaintances. When they failed to find him they went back to Jerusalem looking for him everywhere.

It happened that, three days later, they found him in the Temple, sitting among the teachers, listening to them, and asking them questions; and all those who heard him were astounded at his intelligence and his replies. They were overcome when they saw him, and his mother said to him, 'My child, why have you done this to us? See how worried your father and I have been, looking for you.' He replied, 'Why were you looking for me? Did you not know that I must be in my Father's house?' But they did not understand what he meant.

He went down with them then and came to Nazareth and lived under their authority. His mother stored up all these things in her heart. (Luke 2:41-51, NJB)

And Jesus advanced in wisdom and age and favor before God and man. (Luke 2:52, NAB)

The Sorrowful Mysteries
1. The Agony in the Garden

They came to a plot of land called Gethsemane, and he said to his disciples, 'Stay here while I pray.' Then he took Peter and James and John with him. And he began to feel terror and anguish. And he said to them, 'My soul is sorrowful to the point of death. Wait here, and stay awake.' And going on a little further he threw himself on the ground and prayed that, if it were possible, this hour might pass him by. 'Abba, Father!' he said, 'For you everything is possible. Take this cup away from me. But let it be as you, not I, would have it.' He came back and found them sleeping, and he said to Peter, 'Simon, are you asleep? Had you not the strength to stay awake one hour? Stay awake and pray not to be put to the test. The spirit is willing enough, but human nature is weak.' Again he went away and prayed, saying the same words. (Mark 14:32-39, NJB)

And to strengthen him an angel from heaven appeared to him. He was in such agony and he prayed so fervently that his sweat became like drops of blood falling on the ground. When he rose from prayer and returned to his disciples, he found them sleeping from grief. He said to them, "Why are you sleeping? Get up and pray that you may not undergo the test." (Luke 22:43-46, NAB)

2. The Scourging at the Pillar

'Truth?' said Pilate. 'What is that?' And so saying he went out again to the Jews and said, 'I find no case against him. But according to a custom of yours I should release one prisoner at the Passover; would you like me, then, to release for you the king of the Jews?' At this they shouted, 'Not this man,' they said, 'but Barabbas.' Barabbas was a bandit.

Pilate then had Jesus taken away and scourged. (John 18:38 - 19:1, NJB)

3. The Crowning with Thorns

Then the governor's soldiers took Jesus with them into the Praetorium and collected the whole cohort round him. And they stripped him and put a scarlet cloak round him, and having twisted some thorns into a crown they put this on his head and placed a reed in his right hand. To make fun of him they knelt to him saying, 'Hail, king of the Jews!' And they spat on him and took the reed and struck him on the head with it. (Matthew 27:27-30, NJB)

4. The Carrying of the Cross

As they led him away they took hold of a certain Simon, a Cyrenian, who was coming in from the country; and after laying the cross on him, they made him carry it behind Jesus. A large crowd of people followed Jesus, including many women who mourned and lamented him. Jesus turned to them and said, "Daughters of Jerusalem, do not weep for me; weep instead for yourselves and for your children, for indeed, the days are coming when people will say, 'Blessed are the barren, the wombs that never bore and the breasts that never nursed.' At that time people will say to the mountains, 'Fall upon us!' and to the hills, 'Cover us!' for if these things are done when the wood is green what will happen when it is dry?" (Luke 23:26-31, NAB)

5. The Crucifixion and Death of Jesus

When they reached the place called The Skull, there they crucified him and the two criminals, one on his right, the other on his left. Jesus said, 'Father, forgive them; they do not know what they are doing.' Then they cast lots to share out his clothing.

The people stayed there watching. As for the leaders, they jeered at him with the words, 'He saved others, let him save himself if he is the Christ of God, the Chosen One.' The soldiers mocked him too, coming up to him, offering him vinegar, and saying, 'If you are the king of the Jews, save yourself.' Above him there was an inscription: 'This is the King of the Jews.'

One of the criminals hanging there abused him: 'Are you not the Christ? Save yourself and us as well.' But the other spoke up and rebuked him. 'Have you no fear of God at all?' he said. 'You got the same sentence as he did, but in our case we deserved it: we are paying for what we did. But this man has done nothing wrong.' Then he said, 'Jesus, remember me when you come into your kingdom.' He answered him, 'In truth I tell you, today you will be with me in paradise.' (Luke 23:33-43, NJB)

Near the cross of Jesus stood his mother and his mother's sister, Mary the wife of Clopas, and

Mary of Magdala. Seeing his mother and the disciple whom he loved standing near her, Jesus said to his mother, 'Woman, this is your son.' Then to the disciple he said, 'This is your mother.' And from that hour the disciple took her into his home. (John 19:25-27, NJB)

When the sixth hour came there was darkness over the whole land until the ninth hour. And at the ninth hour Jesus cried out in a loud voice, 'Eloi, eloi, lama sabachthani?' which means, 'My God, my God, why have you forsaken me?' (Mark 15:33-34, NJB)

After this, Jesus knew that everything had now been completed and, so that the scripture should be completely fulfilled, he said:

  I am thirsty.

A jar full of sour wine stood there; so, putting a sponge soaked in the wine on a hyssop stick, they held it up to his mouth. After Jesus had taken the wine he said, 'It is fulfilled.' (John 19:28-30, NJB)

Jesus cried out in a loud voice saying, "Father, into your hands I commit my spirit." With these words he breathed his last. (Luke 23:46, NJB)

And suddenly, the veil of the Sanctuary was torn in two from top to bottom, the earth quaked, the rocks were split, the tombs opened and the bodies of many holy people rose from the dead, and these, after his resurrection, came out of the tombs, entered the holy city and appeared to a number of people. The centurion, together with the others guarding Jesus, had seen the earthquake and all that was taking place, and they were terrified and said, 'In truth this man was son of God.'

And many women were there, watching from a distance, the same women who had followed Jesus from Galilee and looked after him. Among them were Mary of Magdala, Mary the mother of James and Joseph, and the mother of Zebedee's sons. (Matthew 27:51-56, NJB)

It was the Day of Preparation, and to avoid the bodies' remaining on the cross during the Sabbath — since that Sabbath was a day of special solemnity — the Jews asked Pilate to have the legs broken and the bodies taken away. Consequently the soldiers came and broke the legs of the first man who had been crucified with him and then of the other. When they came to Jesus, they saw he was already dead, and so instead of breaking his legs, one of the soldiers pierced his side with a lance; and immediately there came out blood and water. (John 19:31-34, NJB)

1. The Resurrection

The Glorious Mysteries

1. The Resurrection

After the sabbath, as the first day of the week was dawning, Mary Magdalene and the other Mary came to see the tomb. And behold, there was a great earthquake; for an angel of the Lord descended from heaven, approached, rolled back the stone, and sat upon it. His appearance was like lightning and his clothing was white as snow. The guards were shaken with fear of him and became like dead men. Then the angel said to the women in reply, "Do not be afraid! I know that you are seeking Jesus the crucified. He is not here, for he has been raised just as he said. Come and see the place where he lay. Then go quickly and tell his disciples, 'He has been raised from the dead, and he is going before you to Galilee; there you will see him.' Behold, I have told you." Then they went away quickly from the tomb, fearful yet overjoyed, and ran to announce this to his disciples. And behold, Jesus met them on their way and greeted them. They approached, embraced his feet, and did him homage. Then Jesus said to them, "Do not be afraid. Go tell my brothers to go to Galilee, and there they will see me." (Matthew 28: 1-10, NAB)

In the evening of that same day, the first day of the week, the doors were closed in the room where the disciples were, for fear of the Jews. Jesus came and stood among them. He said to them, 'Peace be with you,' and, after saying this, he showed them his hands and his side. The disciples were filled with joy at seeing the Lord, and he said to them again, 'Peace be with you.

'As the Father sent me, so am I sending you.'

After saying this be breathed on them and said:

Receive the Holy Spirit. If you forgive anyone's sins, they are forgiven; if you retain anyone's sins, they are retained.

Thomas, called the Twin, who was one of the Twelve, was not with them when Jeus came. So the other disciples said to him, 'We have seen the Lord,' but he answered, 'Unless I can see the holes that the nails made in his hands and can put my finger into the holes they made, and unless I can put my hand into his side, I refuse to believe.' Eight days later the disciples were in the house again and Thomas was with them. The doors were closed, but Jesus came in and stood among them. 'Peace be with you,' he said. Then he spoke to Thomas, 'Put your finger here; look, here are my hands. Give me your hand; put it into my side. Do not be unbelieving any more but believe.' Thomas replied, 'My Lord and my God!' Jesus said to him:

You believe because you can see me. Blessed are those who have not seen and yet believe. (John 20:19-29, NJB)

Then he told them, 'This is what I meant when I said, while I was still with you, that everything written about me in the Law of Moses, in the Prophets and in the Psalms, was destined to be fulfilled.' He then opened their minds to understand the scriptures, and he said to them, 'So it is written that the Christ would suffer and on the third day rise from the dead, and that, in his name, repentance for the forgiveness of sins would be preached to all nations, beginning from Jerusalem. You are witnesses to this.

'And now I am sending upon you what the Father has promised. Stay in the city, then, until you are clothed with the power from on high.' (Luke 24:44-49, NJB)

And he said to them, 'Go out to the whole world; proclaim the gospel to all creation. Whoever believes and is baptised will be saved; whoever does not believe will be condemned. These are the signs that will be associated with believers: in my name they will cast out devils; they will have the gift of tongues; they will pick up snakes in their hands and be unharmed should they drink deadly poison; they will lay their hands on the sick, who will recover.' (Mark 16:15-18, NJB)

Then Jesus approached and said to them, "All power in heaven and on earth has been given to me. Go, therefore, and make disciples of all nations, baptizing them in the name of the Father, and of the Son, and of the holy Spirit, teaching them to observe all that I have commanded you. And behold, I am with you always, until the end of the age." (Matthew 28:18-20, NAB)

2. The Ascension

Now having met together, they asked him, 'Lord, has the time come for you to restore the kingdom to Israel?' He replied, 'It is not for you to know times or dates that the Father has decided by his own authority, but you will receive the power of the Holy Spirit which will come on you, and then you will be my witnesses not only in Jerusalem but throughout Judaea and Samaria, and indeed to earth's remotest end.'

As he said this he was lifted up while they looked on, and a cloud took him from their sight. They were still staring into the sky as he went, when suddenly two men in white were standing beside them, and they said, 'Why are you Galileans standing here looking into the sky? This Jesus who has been taken up from you into heaven will come back in the same way as you have seen him go to heaven.' (Acts 1:6-11, NJB)

They worshipped him and then went back to Jerusalem full of joy; and they were continually in the Temple praising God. (Luke 24:52-53, NJB)

And so the Lord Jesus, after he had spoken to them, was taken up into heaven; there at the right hand of God he took his place, while they, going out, preached everywhere, the Lord working with them and confirming the word by the signs that accompanied it. (Mark 16:19-20, NJB)

3. The Descent of the Holy Spirit

When Pentecost day came round, they had all met together, when suddenly there came from heaven a sound as of a violent wind which filled the entire house in which they were sitting; and there appeared to them tongues as of fire; these separated and came to rest on the head of each of them. They were all filled with the Holy Spirit and began to speak different languages as the Spirit gave them power to express themselves.

Now there were devout men living in Jerusalem from every nation under heaven, and at this sound they all assembled, and each one was bewildered to hear these men speaking his own language... Everyone was amazed and perplexed; they asked one another what it all meant. Some, however, laughed it off. 'They have been drinking too much new wine,' they said.

Then Peter stood up with the Eleven and addressed them in a loud voice:

'Men of Judaea, and all you who live in Jerusalem, make no mistake about this, but listen carefully to what I say. These men are not drunk, as you imagine; why, it is only the third hour of the day. On the contrary, this is what the prophet was saying:

In the last days — the Lord declares — I shall pour out my Spirit on all humanity. Your sons and daughters shall prophesy, your young people shall see visions, your old people dream dreams. Even on the slaves, men and women, shall I pour out my Spirit...

'Men of Israel, listen to what I am going to say: Jesus the Nazarene was a man commended to you by God by the miracles and portents and signs that God worked through him when he was among you, as you know. This man, who was put into your power by the deliberate intention and foreknowledge of God, you took and had crucified and killed by men outside the Law. But God raised him to life...

'Now raised to the heights by God's right hand, he has received from the Father the Holy Spirit, who was promised, and what you see and hear is the outpouring of that Spirit...'

Hearing this, they were cut to the heart and said to Peter and the other apostles, 'What are we to do, brothers?' 'You must repent,' Peter answered, 'and every one of you must be baptised in the name of Jesus Christ for the forgiveness of your sins, and you will receive the gift of the Holy Spirit. The promise that was made is for you and your children, and for all those who are far away, for all those whom the Lord our God is calling to himself.' He spoke to them for a long time using many other arguments, and he urged them, 'Save yourselves from this perverse generation.' They accepted what he said and were baptised. That very day about three thousand were added to their number. (Acts 2:1-41, NJB)

4. The Assumption of Mary into Heaven

"Finally the Immaculate Virgin, preserved free from all stain of original sin, when the course of her earthly life was finished, was taken up body and soul into heavenly glory..." The Assumption of the Blessed Virgin is a singular participation in her Son's Resurrection and an anticipation of the resurrection of other Christians:

In giving birth you kept your virginity; in your Dormition you did not leave the world, O Mother of God, but were joined to the source of Life. You conceived the living God and, by your prayers, will deliver our souls from death.

(*Catechism of the Catholic Church*: #966)

5. The Coronation of Mary as Queen of Heaven and Earth

"Finally the Immaculate Virgin ... was ... exalted by the Lord as Queen over all things, so that she might be the more fully conformed to her Son, the Lord of lords and conqueror of sin and death." (*Catechism of the Catholic Church*: #966)

Chapter Four

How to Pray the Rosary

Gratitude and joy: these are two richly beneficial attitudes to have while praying. To promote them it is useful to smile throughout the devotion; and we can initiate a smile by squinting the eyes a little while keeping the face and mouth relaxed.

At the same time we should ask the Holy Spirit to help us perceive the kindness with which God looks at his people. May we sense his compassion and love.

Suggestions

Merely reiterating the words of the "Our Father", "Hail Mary" and "Glory Be" is not the best way to pray. At the beginning of each decade, we should take at least fifteen seconds to focus on the announced Mystery.

The following are things we can do during the recitation. We can stay with one of the recommendations over the entire prayer, or use a combination of a few of them.

1. The Scripture quotations associated with each decade of the Rosary is where the most material for meditation is found. As we name each Mystery, let us read a short paragraph from the related texts found in Chapter Three of this booklet, if it is close at hand; if not, let us try to bring one item to mind: a word, a phrase, a sentence, a story, an idea, a deed done by one of the persons described in the incident, a saying uttered by him or her.

2. On days when we are sluggish and dry, and the booklet is not available, we may not be favourably inclined to remember anything significant from the excerpts. In that case we should at least recall the picture that is printed with each Mystery in Chapter Three.

Alternatively, we might see in our mind's eyes a similar image from another book, a stained glass window, a painting, a statue, a holy card. The depiction may be about various parts of the narrative. For instance, in the first Glorious Mystery, the setting may be: Jesus' resurrection at the sepulchre, or the terrified guards, or Peter and John at the empty tomb, Mary Magdalene meeting Jesus in the garden, the doubting Thomas, the road to Emmaus, the draught of fish, Jesus and the apostles on the shore of the lake.

If we wish, we can insert ourselves in the scene — as an onlooker or as one of the participants. There are usually several people in each of the Mysteries: relatives, rabbis, apostles, followers, soldiers, women, passers-by, angels. We can stand in as one of them. Even in the first Joyful Mystery where Mary was presumably alone with the angel Gabriel, we can take the role of her father or mother who could have been in the next room wondering to whom she was talking.

3. Sometimes we can imagine what Jesus could have been feeling, or thinking or saying to himself. For instance, in the fourth Sorrowful Mystery, the Carrying of the Cross, we might 'hear' the exhausted Jesus whispering, "I mustn't give up. I have to go on. My people need me. (George's) son needs me. (Joan's) daughter will not reach heaven if I call it off now." The names in brackets would be replaced by yours.

We may also imagine what another character in the Gospel story could have felt or contemplated. For example, in the fifth Sorrowful Mystery, at the time when the chief priests and scribes were mocking the crucified Jesus, the beloved disciple who was standing near the cross might have asked himself, "Why doesn't He retaliate?" What might have been his answers?

4. We can allude to relevant verses found in a different book of the Bible.

For the second Glorious Mystery, the Ascension, even though it is about Jesus going up to heaven, his assurance should never be forgotten: "I am with you always." (Matthew 28:20, NAB)

5. We may take the opportunity to give God all honour, glory, praise, reverence, love, thanks and adoration.

6. We may wish to ask for a favour, for assistance in overcoming temptations, for solution of a problem, for someone's healing, for the destruction of an evil situation, for our parish priest. We may want to pray for Our Lady's intentions, for the souls in Purgatory, for victims in a disaster, for refugees, for the conversion of sinners, world peace, the well-being of the young, an increase in vocations.

Jesus said, "I came so that they might have life and have it more abundantly." (John 10: 10, NAB)

7. We may explore and emulate a virtue exemplified in the Mystery — like the obedience of Mary in the first and fourth Joyful Mysteries.

8. We may make a special commitment. For example, we may resolve to be firmer in our response to Jesus' call for unwavering faith.

In the third Glorious Mystery, we may promise to be more conscious of the Holy Spirit who lives in us as his temple.

9. We can read the words of introduction to the Mysteries written by holy people like St. Dominic, Blessed Alan de la Roche, St. Louis Marie de Montfort, etc.

We may also listen to recordings of priests, religious or lay persons leading the Rosary.

10. We can think about what is expressed in the "Our Father", the "Hail Mary", the "Glory Be", the Fatima Prayer, the Creed, the "Hail Holy Queen", the fifteen promises.

11. We may sing an appropriate hymn. "Immaculate Mary" would be quite suitable for the fifth Glorious Mystery.

12. We can carry on a conversation with God, with Mary, with one of the angels or saints. We can ask them questions.

As in all dialogue, we should listen intently with the heart.

13. Some days we may elect to remain in stillness in the presence and embrace of God the Father, or Jesus, or the Holy Spirit, or Mary. Let our hearts be satisfied by the joy and peace that comes from communion with any one of them.

14. We may reflect on an implication of the Mystery, a lesson learned, an application for life.

In this regard, it is good to examine our consciences. Our personal sins contributed to Jesus having to suffer enormous pain. Let us look for the root causes of our offenses — pride, disobedience of God's laws, selfishness, inordinate attachment to money and pleasure, lack of love for our neighbour, insufficient faith and hope in the Lord.

15. We can dwell on occasions in which the experiences of Jesus are similar to those of ours. Let us consider ways to intensify our imitation of him and our union with him.

Note:

If an insight should come along during private prayer, we may stop and let the thought continue on to its fullness before resuming the Rosary. However, in a group setting, it is better not to spend more than half a minute vocalizing one's stream of words.

The Rosary

For those who do not know, here is the procedure for praying the Rosary.

As can be seen in Chapter Three, the Rosary consists of three sets of Mysteries — Joyful, Sorrowful and Glorious. Each set commemorates five events in the life of Jesus and/or Mary. Each event is introduced by a title, and an element in it is centred upon during the recitation of one "Our Father", ten "Hail Mary"s, one "Glory Be" and the "Fatima Prayer".

Rosary beads are employed to keep count of the prayers for every five of the fifteen Mysteries.

1(a). Begin by making the SIGN OF THE CROSS.

"In the name of the Father, and of the Son, and of the Holy Spirit. Amen."

(b). Say the "CREED".

[On the Rosary beads, indicate this prayer by taking hold of the crucifix.]

"I believe in God, the Father Almighty, creator of heaven and earth. I believe in Jesus Christ, his only Son, our Lord. He was conceived by the power of the Holy Spirit and born of the Virgin Mary. He suffered under Pontius Pilate, was crucified, died, and was buried. He descended to the dead. On the third day he rose again. He ascended into heaven, and is seated at the right hand of the Father. He will come again to judge the living and the dead. I believe in the Holy Spirit, the holy catholic Church, the communion of saints, the forgiveness of sins, the resurrection of the body, and life everlasting. Amen."

(c). Say the "OUR FATHER".

[On the beads, hold the first bead after the crucifix.]

"Our Father, who art in heaven, hallowed be Thy name. Thy kingdom come, Thy will be done on earth as it is in heaven. Give us this day our daily bread, and forgive us our trespasses as we forgive those who trespass against us. And lead us not into temptation, but deliver us from evil. Amen."

(d). Say three times the "HAIL MARY".

[These are counted on the next three beads.]

"Hail Mary, full of grace, the Lord is with thee. Blessed art thou amongst women, and blessed is the fruit of thy womb, Jesus. Holy Mary, Mother of God, pray for us sinners, now and at the hour of our death. Amen."

These three prayers are said for an increase in faith, hope and love.

(e). Say the "GLORY BE".

[This is the last bead before the major part of the Rosary whose 54 beads are chained together in the shape of a loop.]

"Glory be to the Father, and to the Son, and to the Holy Spirit — as it was in the beginning, is now, and ever shall be, world without end. Amen."

2(a). Announce the first Mystery. (Refer to Chapter Three.) Pause a few seconds for reflection as described at the beginning of the present chapter.

(b). Say the "Our Father", the "Hail Mary" ten

times, and the "Glory Be", followed by the "FATIMA PRAYER".

"O my Jesus, forgive us our sins, save us from the fires of hell, lead all souls to heaven, especially those who are most in need of Thy mercy."

(c). Announce the next Mystery, pause a few seconds for reflection, and repeat step (b).

Step (c) recurs until five Mysteries have been completed.

[On the beads the connecting centre piece medal is used to count the first "Our Father" for the first Mystery, and the fifth "Glory Be" and "Fatima Prayer". The sequences of ten beads are for keeping track of the "Hail Mary"s. The single bead after each ten is used for the "Glory Be", the "Fatima Prayer" and the next "Our Father".]

3(a). After finishing five Mysteries, say the "HAIL HOLY QUEEN".

"Hail, holy Queen, Mother of mercy; hail, our life, our sweetness and our hope. To thee do we cry, poor banished children of Eve. To thee we send up our sighs, mourning and weeping in this vale of tears. Turn, then, most gracious

Advocate, thine eyes of mercy towards us, and after this our exile, show unto us the blessed fruit of thy womb, Jesus. O clement, O loving, O sweet Virgin Mary."

(b). Say the final INVOCATION.

"Pray for us, O holy Mother of God. That we may be made worthy of the promises of Christ."

"Let us pray. O God, whose only begotten Son, by his life, death and resurrection, has purchased for us the rewards of eternal salvation, grant, we beseech Thee, that meditating upon these Mysteries in the most holy Rosary of the Blessed Virgin Mary, we may imitate what they contain and obtain what they promise. Through the same Christ, our Lord. Amen."

(c). End by making the "Sign of the Cross" again.

Notes

4. The shorter version of the Rosary consists only of Step 2.

5. If all fifteen Mysteries are prayed in one sitting, then Step 1 occurs only at the beginning, and Step 3 only at the end.

6. If five Mysteries are prayed daily, it is customary to say the Joyful Mysteries on Mondays and Thursdays, the Sorrowful on Tuesdays and Fridays, and the Glorious on Wednesdays and Saturdays. Sundays follow the liturgical calendar — Joyful from Advent to the day before Ash Wednesday, Sorrowful during Lent, and Glorious at Easter and throughout the rest of the year.

7. Dozens of books have been written on the Rosary. The most enduring one was by St. Louis Marie Grignon de Montfort: *The Secret of the Rosary* (Montfort Publications, Bay Shore, N.Y. 11706). In it he gives detailed instructions on many topics — such as the proper dispositions for reciting this prayer, its effects and benefits, etc.

8. The Rosary in its present form was given by Our Lady to St. Dominic (founder of the Dominicans — the Order of Preachers) in France in the early 1200's. Then Blessed Alan de la Roche, a French Dominican, re-established its practice in the mid-1400's. And from the 18th century onwards St. Louis de Montfort became its most famous promoter. He was a French priest in the Third Order of St. Dominic.

9. The word "rosary" means "a crown of roses". A person who says this prayer brings dozens of beautiful roses to a very appreciative Mother.

God said, "Honour your father and your mother." Jesus keeps this commandment. So should we.

10. The 150 Hail Mary's in the full Rosary correspond roughly to the number of psalms that were chanted by the monks to praise God in their monasteries.

11. The Greek word for ten is deka. This is the origin of the term 'decade' which is often used to indicate the ten Hail Mary's recited for each Mystery.

12. The Rosary does not violate Jesus' injunc-

tion: "In praying, do not babble like the pagans, who think that they will be heard because of their many words." (Matthew 6:7, NAB) Jesus is against "babbling", not repetition. At Gethsemane he himself made three identical requests to his Father to let the cup pass him by. "Leaving them there, he went away again and prayed for the third time, repeating the same words." (Matthew 26:44, NJB)

Furthermore, in parables like that of the importunate widow (Luke 18:1-8), Jesus lauds the virtue of persistence.

13. The Rosary is a prayer endorsed and encouraged by the Church. Pope Leo XIII wrote no less than twelve encyclicals on this subject. The devotion is practised, both publicly and in private, by popes, cardinals, bishops, priests, religious, and millions of lay people.

14. The Blessed Virgin Mary, in her recent apparitions on earth, urges everyone to recite this prayer daily. For example, at Fatima, her words were: "Say the Rosary every day to earn peace for the world..."

15. In the liturgical calendar the Church celebrates October 7th as the feastday of Our Lady of the Holy Rosary.

Chapter Five

Indulgences

What is an Indulgence?

For answers, we look to the *Catechism of the Catholic Church* (Publications Service, Canadian Conference of Catholic Bishops, Ottawa, 1994).

"An indulgence is a remission before God of the temporal punishment due to sins whose guilt has already been forgiven, which the faithful Christian who is duly disposed gains under certain prescribed conditions through the action of the Church which, as the minister of redemption, dispenses and applies with authority the treasury of the satisfactions of Christ and the saints." (#1471)

"The 'treasury of the Church' is the infinite value, which can never be exhausted, which Christ's merits have before God. They were offered so that the whole of mankind could be set free from sin and attain communion with the Father." (#1476)

"This treasury includes as well the prayers and good works of the Blessed Virgin Mary. They are truly immense, unfathomable and even pristine in their value before God. In the treasury, too, are the prayers and good works of all the saints." (#1477)

"To understand this doctrine and practice of the Church, it is necessary to understand that sin has a double consequence. Grave sin deprives us of communion with God and therefore makes us incapable of eternal life, the privation of which is called the 'eternal punishment' of sin. On the other hand every sin, even venial, entails an unhealthy attachment to creatures, which must be purified either here on earth, or after death in the state called Purgatory. This purification frees one from what is called the 'temporal punishment' of sin. These two punishments must not be conceived of as a kind of vengeance inflicted by God from without, but as following from the very nature of sin." (#1472)

Purpose and Past Abuses

The remaining parts of this booklet are excerpts taken from *The Handbook of Indulgences, Norms and Grants* (Catholic Book Publishing Co., New York, 1991). The reader is encouraged to study this valuable little work in its entirety.

"The purpose intended by ecclesiastical authority in granting indulgences is not only to help the faithful to pay the penalties due to sin, but also to cause them to perform works of devotion, repentance, and charity - especially works that contribute to the growth of faith and the good of the community.

"The faithful who apply indulgences as suffrages for the dead are practicing charity in a superior way and with their thoughts on the things of heaven are dealing more virtuously with the things of earth.

"The Church's magisterium has defended and declared this teaching in various documents. The practice of indulgences has sometimes been infected with abuses. This has happened because 'rash and excessive indulgences' have led to contempt for the keys of the Church and to the weakening of penitential expiation, and because 'fraudulent appeals for money' have brought curses upon the very name of indulgences. The Church, however, uprooting and correcting abuses, 'teaches and prescribes that the practice of indulgences, so beneficial to the Christian people and sanctioned by the authority of the sacred councils, must be preserved; the Church anathematizes those who state that indulgences are useless or who deny the Church's power to grant them.'" (Pages 112-114)

"In addition, the usage of indulgence builds up confidence and hope for full reconciliation with God the Father. Yet this occurs in such a way that the practice provides no basis for negligence nor in any way lessens the concern to develop those dispositions required for full communion with God. Indulgences are indeed freely given favors, but they are granted both to the living and the dead only on fulfillment of certain conditions: to gain them the requirement on the one hand is the performance of good works, and on the other the faithful's having the necessary dispositions, namely, love of God, hatred toward sin, trust in the merits of Christ the Lord, and the firm belief that the communion of saints is of great advantage to the faithful." (Page 114)

Some Norms
"**2**. An indulgence is either plenary of partial, that is, it frees a person either from all or from some of the temporal punishment due to sins.

"**3**. No one gaining an indulgence may apply it to other living persons.

"**4**. Both partial and plenary indulgences can always be applied to the dead as suffrages.

"**20**. 1. To be capable of gaining indulgences a person must be baptized, not excommunicated, and in the state of grace at least at the time the prescribed works are completed.

"**23**. 1. Beside the exclusion of all attachment to sin, even venial sin, the requirements for gaining a plenary indulgence are the performance of the indulgenced work and fulfillment of three conditions: sacramental confession, eucharistic communion, and prayer for the pope's intentions." (Pages 19-24)

Indulgenced Grants
"48. Recitation of the Marian Rosary

A plenary indulgence is granted when the rosary is recited in a church or oratory or when it is recited in a family, a religious community, or a pious association. A partial indulgence is granted for its recitation in all other circumstances.

1. The recitation of a third of the rosary is sufficient for obtaining the plenary indulgence, but these five decades must be recited without interruption.

2. Devout meditation on the mysteries is to be added to the vocal prayer." (Page 79)

"35. Use of Devotional Objects

The Christian faithful obtain a partial indulgence when they make devout use of a devotional object (such as a crucifix or cross, a rosary, a scapular, or a medal) which has been rightly blessed by any priest or deacon." (Page 74)

"55. Sign of the Cross

A partial indulgence is granted the Christian faithful who devoutly sign themselves with the cross while saying the customary formula: 'In the name of the Father, and of the Son, and of the Holy Spirit. Amen.'" (Page 82)

"16. Creed

A partial indulgence is granted the Christian faithful who devoutly recite the above Apostles' Creed or the Nicene-Constantinopolitan Creed." (Page 49)

"50. Reading the Sacred Scriptures

A partial indulgence is granted the Christian faithful who read sacred scripture with the veneration due God's word and as a form of spiritual reading. The indulgence will be a plenary one when such reading is done for at least one-half hour." (Page 80)

"51. Hail, Holy Queen

A partial indulgence." (Page 81)